A is for America

An American Alphabet

Written by Devin Scillian and Illustrated by Pam Carroll

Sleeping Bear Press™
310 North Main Street, Suite 300
Chelsea, MI 48118
www.sleepingbearpress.com

© 2001 Sleeping Bear Press is an imprint of Gale, a part of Cengage Learning.

Printed and bound in China.

10 9 8 7 6 5 4 3 2 1 (pbk)
10 9 8 7 6 (case)

Library of Congress Cataloging-in-Publication Data
Scillian, Devin.
A is for America / author, Devin Scillian ; illustrator, Pamela Carroll.
p. cm.

pbk ISBN 978-1-58536-425-1
case ISBN 978-1-58536-015-4

1. United States-Juvenile literature. 2. English language-Alphabet-Juvenile literature.
[1. United States-Miscellanea.
2. Alphabet.] I. Carroll, Pamela, ill. II. Title.
E156 .S35 2001
973—dc21   00-012262

For Mom, who taught me to love books, and Dad, who taught me to love my country.

D.S.

To my loving husband Chris, and my beloved son Dustin, thank you for your unwavering belief in my ability as an artist. To my sister Penny, an artist of immense talent, I thank you for your love and creative support. To Kennon, Amy, and Gwendolyn from the Carmel Harrison Memorial Library, whose research was instrumental to me and to this project, I want you to know I could not have done it without you. And finally to my dearest friend Elizabeth, a dedicated teacher who reminded me how much fun it is to look at life through the eyes of a child.

P.C.

The United States of America was formed in 1776 out of 13 colonies that fought for independence from Great Britain. Compared to many nations around the world, the United States is relatively young. It is neither the largest country in the world, nor the most populous. But in so many ways, the United States of America is the most influential nation on earth, especially in its belief in democracy—the idea that a government should be "of the people, by the people, and for the people."

Go tell Matt and Ian and Madison and Bo,
and Griffin, Quinn, and Christian, and everyone you know.
Tell Andy, Bryson, Mason, Kirby, Addison, and Erica.
Shout it from the highest hill that A is for America.

B b

The Battle of Bunker Hill was actually won by the British. But the American patriots fought so bravely that the battle became a rallying cry for the rest of the American Revolution.

The Liberty Bell can be found in Philadelphia. It was rung in 1776 to announce a public reading of the Declaration of Independence.

The Liberty Bell hasn't been rung since 1846 when the bell cracked.

B can be for Boston, and the Battle of Bunker Hill.
    And breaking from the British who ruled here until
a band of brave believers behind a boisterous yell
    brought forth a brand new nation and banged the Liberty Bell.

C is for the cities that reach into the blue,
like Chicago, Cleveland, Charlotte, and Cincinnati do.
And it's for the Constitution that guides us still today,
written for "We the people" to find a better way.

New Cuyahoga County Court House
Cleveland

CHICAGO

We the People

CITIE

C

Cities in the United States come in all sizes and personalities. Each has its own habits and traditions. Charleston, South Carolina is very different from Cheyenne, Wyoming. But they are both very American.

The Constitution is the set of ideas and laws that gave birth to the United States of America. It was written in 1787 and it very much guides our nation today. Many other nations have used the American Constitution as an instruction book for their own governments.

Detroit is in Michigan, a northern state. Dallas is in Texas, a southern state. Denver is in Colorado, a western state. Dover is in Delaware, an eastern state.

There are two Dakotas in the United States, North Dakota and South Dakota. Dakota is the Sioux Indian word for "friend."

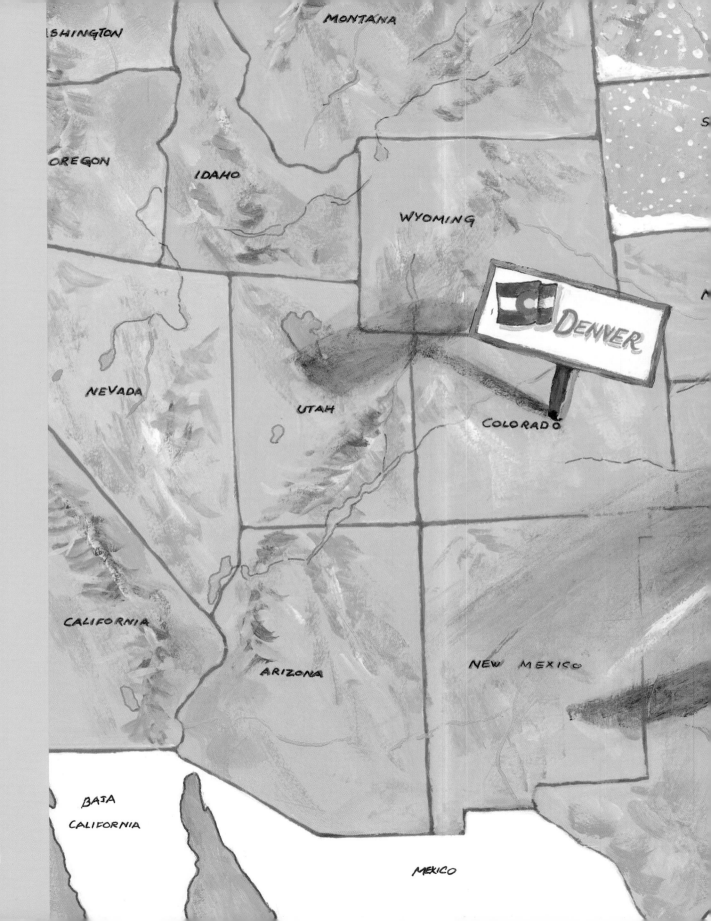

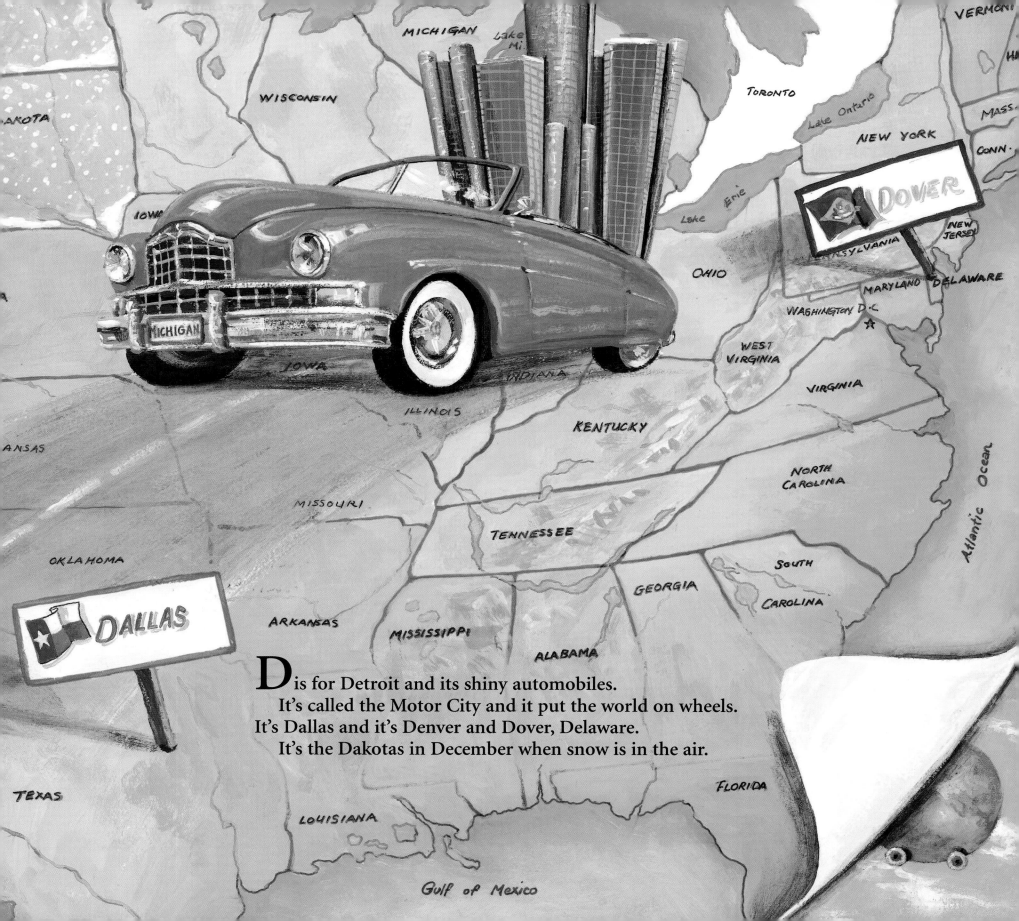

D is for Detroit and its shiny automobiles.
It's called the Motor City and it put the world on wheels.
It's Dallas and it's Denver and Dover, Delaware.
It's the Dakotas in December when snow is in the air.

E is the elegant eagle, soaring above the hill,
and the ever-flowing everglades where egrets eat their fill.
E is an endless echo in the Grand Canyon at dawn.
And eureka! It's Thomas Edison turning the light bulb on.

The bald eagle is the symbol of the United States.

Egrets are tall, slender birds that live in the swamps of Florida, better known as the Everglades.

While Thomas Edison was a brilliant man who invented many things, the light bulb wasn't one of them. While he's given credit for the invention, he actually improved on the designs of others.

E e

We celebrate Independence Day on July 4th of every year.

The fireworks we display remind us of the "rocket's red glare" mentioned in our national anthem, "The Star Spangled Banner."

Phoenix, Arizona is the largest capital city in the United States.

Montpelier, Vermont is the smallest capital city.

f F

F is for the fireworks that fly on the Fourth,
from Ft. Worth in the south to Fargo in the north.
F is fifty fluttering flags and fifty license plates.
Fifty fine state capitals in fifty United States.

G is for gold rush that swept the golden state,
and gave us California with its grand Golden Gate.
And for Alaska's glaciers that glisten on the coast.
And the gushing of a geyser that hovers like a ghost.

"THERE'S GOLD IN THEM HILLS"

The name "California" came from an old Spanish story about an island of gold.

The Golden Gate Bridge in San Francisco is actually painted orange, but it looks golden in the sunlight.

Old Faithful at Yellowstone National Park is perhaps the world's most famous geyser. It erupts about 20 times every day.

Gg

Ernest Hemingway is remembered as one of the greatest writers in American history. His stories were filled with adventure.

The Adventures of Huckleberry Finn was written by Mark Twain. It's about an orphaned boy living along the Mississippi River in the 1800s.

Henry Ford didn't invent the automobile. But his way of building them was so successful many people believe he did.

H stands for Hemingway and Huckleberry Finn,
hydroelectric Hoover Dam and so many Holiday Inns.
Hot dogs and Hawaii, Henry Ford and his cars.
Heading home on Halloween with chocolate Hershey bars.

Freedom of Religion
Freedom of Speech
Freedom of
Freedom
Free
Fr

I is indeed important, how America came to be.
It's the idea that an individual can insist on being free.
And I is for immigration and the immigrants who came
from Italy, Ireland or India, we're Americans all the same.

Most early settlers who came to the United States were looking for some kind of freedom—to work, worship, or live as they wished.

Many immigrants who came to America made their first stop at Ellis Island, New York, where they were allowed into the United States to begin their new lives.

The Statue of Liberty has become a symbol of freedom to people all over the world. Lady Liberty stands in New York Harbor.

I i

Jamestown, Virginia was one of the first permanent settlements in America.

Thomas Jefferson is remembered as one of the greatest Americans in history. He was a patriot, a philosopher, a statesman, a farmer, a musician, a diplomat, and an architect.

Wyoming was home to Chief Washakie, a Shoshone chief who became the first Native American buried with full U.S. military honors.

In jazz, musicians are free to make up the music as they go along. This "improvisational" music most likely got its start in New Orleans.

Jj

From Jamestown to James Monroe, we need the letter J.
If not for Thomas Jefferson, where would we be today?
It's Jackson Hole, Wyoming and the jiggle that Jell-O has.
It's a jam session jumping with the music we call jazz.

Kitty Hawk and Kansas, and Kodiak bears.
King Kamehameha, Kellogg's Rice Krispies squares.
K is for two kinds of King—George the Third who was defeated,
and Martin Luther Junior whom our troubled nation needed.

Kitty Hawk, North Carolina is where Orville and Wilbur Wright flew the very first airplane. The first flight took place December 17, 1903 and lasted 12 seconds.

King Kamehameha was the ruler of Hawaii more than 100 years before Hawaii became a state.

The birthday of civil rights leader Martin Luther King, Jr. was established as a national holiday in 1983.

K
k

While Abraham Lincoln was president, the United States was in danger of splitting into two countries.

In 1863, he issued the Emancipation Proclamation which ended slavery.

For keeping the nation together in such troubled times, many historians believe Abraham Lincoln was the greatest president in American history.

IN THIS TEMPLE
AS IN THE HEARTS OF THE PEOPLE
FOR WHOM HE SAVED THE UNION
THE MEMORY OF ABRAHAM LINCOLN
IS ENSHRINED FOREVER

L1

Abraham Lincoln gets all of L. It's elementary you see.
He held us all together and at the same time set us free.
His memorial in Washington makes him a giant of a man.
Or look upon a smaller one—the penny in your hand.

M Mayflower, Minuteman, Motown, manatee.
is Mickey Mantle, Mickey Mouse, Monopoly.
M can seem so mighty when it's a river rolling by.
M-I-S-S-I-S-S-I-P-P-I.

One of the greatest baseball players ever, Mickey Mantle was named for another great player, Mickey Cochrane.

The manatee is sometimes called a "sea cow."

The Mississippi River is the longest river in the U.S., stretching from Lake Itasca, Minnesota to just south of New Orleans, Louisiana.

Motown introduced the world to many amazingly talented African American musicians and performers.

M
m

Perhaps the country's most beloved artist, Norman Rockwell painted everyday scenes of American life.

More than 400 Native Americans from the Navaho (Navajo) tribe helped the United States win World War II with the Navaho language. Troop movements and battle plans were communicated through Navaho "code talkers." The enemy was unable to decipher what the code talkers were saying.

In 1969, the entire world watched as Neil Armstrong became the first man to set foot on the moon. Joining him on the Apollo 11 mission were Buzz Aldrin and Michael Collins.

Norman Rockwell, Niagara Falls, a night in New Mexico.
New Orleans and Native American. N is for Navaho.
And NASA and Neil Armstrong, who reached the moon to find
that it was one small step for man, one giant leap for mankind.

The Old West, the OK Corral, the old Oregon Trail.
An old ornery outlaw, an owl on a rail.
Old Faithful, Old Glory, and good old Oreos.
An overlook in the Ozarks where the occasional opossum goes.

O o

The OK Corral was the site of a famous gunfight in Tombstone, Arizona in 1881.

The Oregon Trail was actually a series of trails that allowed settlers to move from the eastern half of the country to the western half.

Old Glory is a nickname for the U.S. flag.

Pp

Pikes Peak was named for Zebulon Pike whose only attempt at climbing the mountain was unsuccessful due to a storm.

Peanut butter was just one of more than 300 uses for peanuts invented by George Washington Carver.

Rosa Parks helped the nation understand that rights were for everyone, regardless of their skin color.

Pikes Peak and peanut butter—that's the letter P.
Plymouth Rock and pilgrims at peril on the sea.
Rosa Parks, parades, popcorn in a pan.
Philadelphia, Pennsylvania where all of it began.

Qis for the quill that John Hancock used to place
his quite creative signature in a most important space.
It's for the American quarter, and the bobwhite quail
and the quilts that kept the Quakers warm in a Pennsylvania gale.

John Hancock was the President of the Second Continental Congress, which drew up the Declaration of Independence. His large and unique signature on the Declaration of Independence became so famous that today someone may request your signature by asking for your "John Hancock."

Many Quakers came to America seeking religious freedom. Many settled in Pennsylvania which was named for a Quaker, William Penn.

Q q

A remote reach of the Rockies, the reflection of Mt. Rainier.
The regal ridge of Mt. Rushmore, the ride of Paul Revere.
The Roosevelts, Franklin and Teddy, Babe Ruth, rock and roll.
Rosie the Riveter, the Rio Grande, and "remember the Alamo."

R r

The Rocky Mountains stretch from New Mexico to Alaska.

The faces of four presidents are carved on Mt. Rushmore: George Washington, Thomas Jefferson, Abraham Lincoln, and Theodore Roosevelt.

Rosie the Riveter symbolizes the role that women played in keeping the U.S.A. strong during World War II.

Old Glory isn't the only nickname for the U.S. flag. It's also known as the Stars and Stripes.

There are 13 stripes on the flag, one for each of the original colonies. And there are 50 stars on the flag, one for each state.

Susan B. Anthony crusaded for women's rights, including the right to vote.

Sitting Bull was a great chief of the Sioux Indians.

S s

Stand and salute the Stars and Stripes, a symbol to celebrate.
A stripe for each of the colonies and a star for every state.
Susan B. Anthony, Sierra Nevada, a steam locomotive train.
Sitting Bull and Samuel Clemens, better known as Mark Twain.

A **T** as tall as Texas for Thanksgiving and telephone.
Harry S. Truman, Harriet Tubman, and trips to the Twilight Zone.
Times Square on New Year's Eve, a tasty Tootsie Roll.
Turning timber into a tall and towering totem pole.

The tradition of Thanksgiving began with the Pilgrims before the United States was even a country. It's now celebrated on the fourth Thursday of November.

Born into slavery, Harriet Tubman freed herself and then worked to free many, many others.

Times Square in New York City hosts the world's most famous New Year's Eve Party every December 31st.

The name "Utah" comes from a Native American word meaning "people of the mountains."

Ulysses S. Grant was the commander of the Union Army in the Civil War. After the war, he became the country's 18th President.

Written by Harriet Beecher Stowe, *Uncle Tom's Cabin* taught much of the nation about slavery.

U takes us up to Utah, unafraid of an upcoming storm.
It's undeniably Ulysses S. Grant in his Union uniform.
It's also *Uncle Tom's Cabin* which helped us understand
the uncommon things we must uphold for dear old Uncle Sam.

V is for the veterans and the valor they displayed
in vying for vital victories and the sacrifices they made.
V is for Virginia and Vermont and Vikings, too.
It seems they got here long before Columbus was able to.

ST. JOHN'S CHURCH

RICHMOND, VIRGINIA

Vermont

Veterans are people who have served their country in the armed forces. Many people gave their lives fighting for the United States of America.

Four of the first five Presidents were born in Virginia (George Washington, Thomas Jefferson, James Madison, and James Monroe).

While Christopher Columbus often gets the credit, it's now believed that Viking Leif Ericson was the first European to reach North America.

V
v

W
W

After leading the American armies in the Revolution, George Washington became the first president of the United States.

Washington was the first man to sign the Constitution of the United States of America.

George Washington is the only U.S. president who didn't live in the White House. It wasn't completed until after he left office.

Washington believed he was first and foremost a farmer. He introduced the mule to American farming.

Wheeling, West Virginia, Walt Disney, a wagon train.
World War I and World War II, the World Series and John Wayne.
W stands for Washington, who wintered at Valley Forge.
City, state, and president, all named for him, by George.

Suspension Bridge. Wheeling, W. Va.

WORLD WAR I

48 ADMIT

WORLD SERIES

The letter **X** should remind us of the importance of election day,
when all Americans rich and poor are allowed to have their say.
Some were told they couldn't vote if they couldn't write their name.
So they signed the ballot with a letter X and it counted just the same.

Free elections are one of the most cherished and important practices of a democracy.

Early in our nation's history, only white men were allowed to vote. But amendments to our Constitution gave voting rights to men and women of every race.

Local elections are held at various times, but national elections are held on the first Tuesday in November.

X
X
X

Yy

Yellowstone National Park is located mostly in Wyoming, but extends into Montana and Idaho as well.

Yosemite National Park is located in the Sierra Nevada Mountains of California.

The New York Yankees are probably the most famous sports team in American history.

Y can make you hungry, as Yogi Bear has shown.
Out yonder you'll find Y for Yosemite and Yellowstone.
The Y can be a place for fun like the YMCA.
And in the Bronx it's Yankee Stadium where the New York Yankees play.

Z is for Zane Grey who wrote stories about the west.
Z is also for ZIP codes, but I think that I like best
for Z to remind us of Whitcomb Judson as clever as he could be.
He gave us the magical zipper in 1893.

Air Mail

CHICAGO ILLINOIS
AUG.
29
1938
U.S.A POSTAGE

Whitcomb Judson
Chicago
IL 60601

The Last of the Plainsmen

Zane Grey
Zanesville, Ohio

ZANESVILLE, OHIO
JAN.
31
1932
U.S POSTAGE

3 U.S. POSTAGE
VIA AIR MAIL

43701

It's a special place, this land of ours,
from sea to shining sea.
And now you know it from America's A
all the way to zipper's Z.

The United States Post Office added ZIP codes to mailing addresses in 1963.

Whitcomb Judson actually called his invention a "clasp locker." And it wasn't designed for clothes. It was originally designed to replace shoestrings on shoes.

Fourteen years after Judson's death, the B.F. Goodrich Company began calling his device a "zipper" because of the way it sounded.

Zz

Oh, say can you see, by the dawn's early light,
What so proudly we hailed at the twilight's last gleaming?
Whose broad stripes and bright stars, through the perilous fight,
O'er the ramparts we watched, were so gallantly streaming?
And the rocket's red glare, the bombs bursting in air,
Gave proof through the night that our flag was still there.
O say, does that star-spangled banner yet wave
O'er the land of the free and the home of the brave?

During the War of 1812, Major George Armistead, the commander of Fort McHenry on the coast of Maryland, wanted a flag that would be visible from a distance to enemies. A committee of high-ranking officials called on the sewing skills of Mary Young Pickersgill, a Baltimore widow known for her work on ships' flags. They asked for an American flag that measured 30 feet by 42 feet, and she agreed to take on the job.

Mrs. Pickersgill, along with her 13-year-old daughter Caroline, spent several weeks measuring, cutting, and sewing various pieces of the flag together. When it came time to assemble the entire flag, however, they realized that their home was not large enough. The owner of a local brewery agreed to let the women use his building in the evenings, where they worked by candlelight to finish the flag.

In 1814, lawyer Francis Scott Key was waiting on a ship offshore from Fort McHenry, escorting a doctor whose release he had just secured from a British ship. The British began firing on Fort McHenry, a battle that lasted through a rainy night. The next morning, Francis Scott Key witnessed the raising of Mrs. Pickersgill's flag.

Realizing the fort had not fallen to the British, and thrilled by the sight of that flag, Key was inspired to write the lyrics that would become "The Star Spangled Banner." The actual flag that flew that morning can be seen in the Mall entrance to the Smithsonian Museum in Washington, D.C.